Dear Parent:

Congratulations! Your child is taking the first steps on an exciting journey. The destination? Independent reading!

STEP INTO READING® will help your child get there. The program offers five steps to reading success. Each step includes fun stories and colorful art. There are also Step into Reading Sticker Books, Step into Reading Math Readers, Step into Reading Write-In Readers, Step into Reading Phonics Readers, and Step into Reading Phonics First Steps! Boxed Sets—a complete literacy program with something for every child.

Learning to Read, Step by Step!

Ready to Read Preschool–Kindergarten
• big type and easy words • rhyme and rhythm • picture clues
For children who know the alphabet and are eager to begin reading.

Reading with Help Preschool–Grade 1
• basic vocabulary • short sentences • simple stories
For children who recognize familiar words and sound out new words with help.

Reading on Your Own Grades 1–3
• engaging characters • easy-to-follow plots • popular topics
For children who are ready to read on their own.

Reading Paragraphs Grades 2–3
• challenging vocabulary • short paragraphs • exciting stories
For newly independent readers who read simple sentences with confidence.

Ready for Chapters Grades 2–4
• chapters • longer paragraphs • full-color art
For children who want to take the plunge into chapter books but still like colorful pictures.

STEP INTO READING® is designed to give every child a successful reading experience. The grade levels are only guides. Children can progress through the steps at their own speed, developing confidence in their reading, no matter what their grade.

Remember, a lifetime love of reading starts with a single step!

To Zachary, who likes bugs
—G.B.K.

Text copyright © 1954, renewed 1982 by Random House, Inc. Illustrations copyright © 1999
by G. Brian Karas. Afterword copyright © 1999 by Leonard S. Marcus. All rights reserved
under International and Pan-American Copyright Conventions. Published in the United States
by Random House Children's Books, a division of Random House, Inc., New York, and
simultaneously in Canada by Random House of Canada Limited, Toronto. Originally published
in slightly different form by Golden Books, an imprint of Random House Children's Books, a
division of Random House, Inc., in 1954. This revised edition originally published by Golden
Books in 1999.

www.stepintoreading.com

Educators and librarians, for a variety of teaching tools, visit us at
www.randomhouse.com/teachers

Library of Congress Cataloging-in-Publication Data
Brown, Margaret Wise, 1910–1952.
I like bugs / by Margaret Wise Brown ; illustrated by G. Brian Karas ; with an afterword by
Leonard S. Marcus.   p.   cm. — (Step into reading. A step 1 book)
Originally published: New York : Golden Books, c1999.
SUMMARY: In brief rhyming text, lists all the types of insects the narrator likes.
ISBN 0-307-26107-7 (pbk.) — ISBN 0-307-46107-6 (lib. bdg.)
[1. Insects—Fiction.   2. Stories in rhyme.]
I. Karas, G. Brian, ill.   II. Title.   III. Series: Step into reading. Step 1 book.   PZ8.3.H848   Ph
2003   [E]—dc21   2002013565

Printed in the United States of America   25 24 23
First Random House Edition
STEP INTO READING, RANDOM HOUSE, and the Random House colophon are registered trademarks
of Random House, Inc.

I Like Bugs

By Margaret Wise Brown
Illustrated by G. Brian Karas
With an afterword by Leonard S. Marcus

Random House 🏠 New York

I like bugs.

Black bugs.

Green bugs.

Bad bugs.

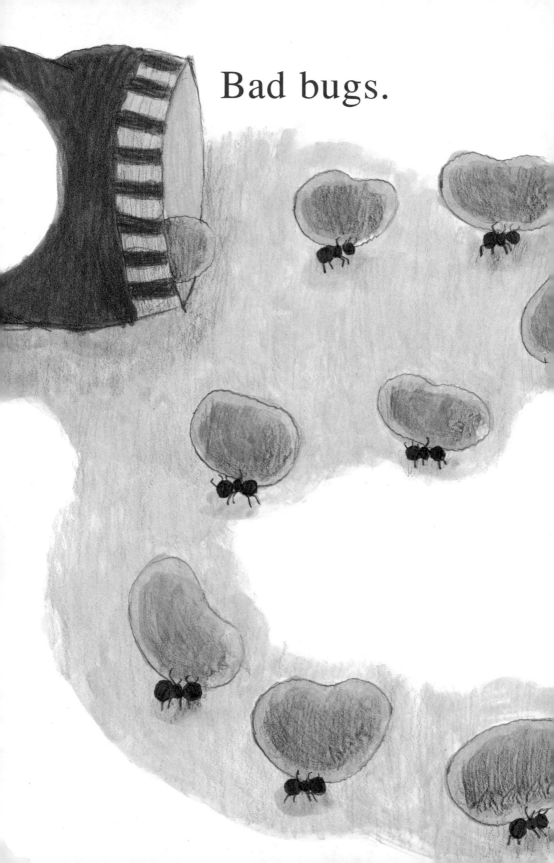

Mean bugs.

Any kind of bug.

A bug in a rug.

A bug in the grass.

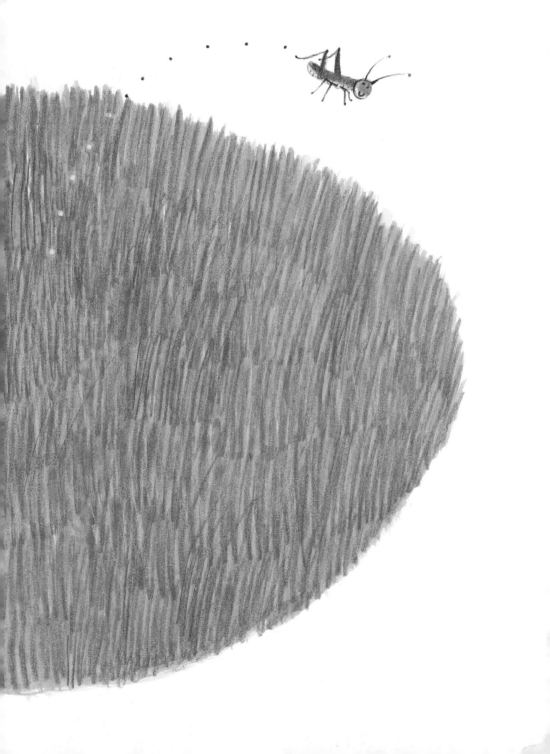

A bug on the sidewalk.

A bug in a glass.

I like bugs.

Round bugs.

Shiny bugs.

Fat bugs.

Buggy bugs.

Big bugs.

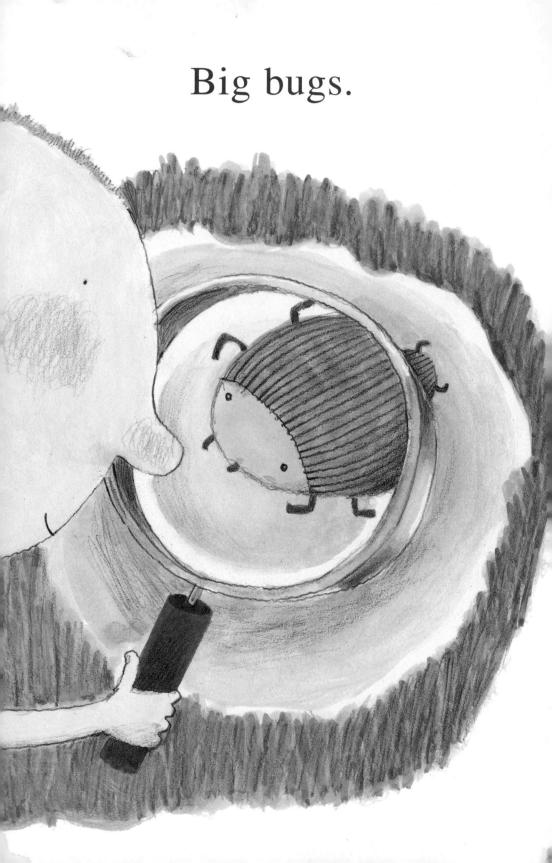

Lady bugs.

I like bugs.

About the Author

Margaret Wise Brown liked bugs. In summertime as a child, she liked to catch fireflies after dark. Margaret and her younger sister, Roberta, would bring the magical bugs indoors and fall asleep watching them blink on and off like stars. A star show in a jar!

Margaret liked to listen to bugs. As an author, she put the sounds that bugs make—the bee's *Bzzzzzzz* and the cricket's *Ticka ticka ticka ticka*—into her stories and poems. In *The Country Noisy Book* she

slyly hints that when the katydid—
a cricket-like insect—rubs its wings
together to produce its very own
shrill sound, it is telling us a story.
*Katydid katydidn't katydid
katydidn't.*

Margaret liked to watch bugs,
too. Watching with her keen, quick
gray-green eyes, she saw the colors
and shapes of the bugs around her.
She saw the ladybug's polka-dot
pattern and the beetle's shiny back.

In *I Like Bugs*, she tells about
many kinds of bugs: black bugs,
green ones, bad bugs, mean ones.
But have you ever met a bad bug?

Do you think you'd like it if you did?

Most of all, Margaret Wise Brown liked bugs because they are bugs: a part of our world and a part of the "wild green world" of nature.

What kind of bug is your favorite?

–Leonard S. Marcus

Leonard S. Marcus is a well-known biographer and historian, and the author of Margaret Wise Brown: Awakened by the Moon.